D1002746

To: _Harold Howard_

From: _Jerry & Jennifer_

"You can have everything in life you want, if you will just help enough other people get what they want."

Zig Ziglar

I am often asked what my favorite quote or saying is. Frankly, there are hundreds of inspiring adages that help illustrate the incredible potential each of us possesses. I hope this Little Book Of Quotes will inspire, encourage and motivate you, provide hope and at times a smile.

I trust you will find them insightful and in some context, useful. I hope they make you think, give you new ideas, and extract more of the potential in you.

I am also hopeful that they will collectively reveal a philosophy. In what is essentially an interpretation of the Golden Rule, it is my sincere belief that you can have everything in life you want if you will just help enough other people get what they want.

See You Over the Top,

Zig Ziglar

Ambition

Ambition

Your business is never really good or bad "out there."
Your business is either good or bad
right between your own two ears.

The real opportunity for success
lies within the person and not in the job.

It is easy to get to the top after you get
through the crowd at the bottom.

Success is not a destination, it's a journey.

The most practical, beautiful, workable philosophy
in the world won't work – if you won't.

Motivation is the fuel necessary
to keep the human engine running.

Discipline yourself to do the things you need to do
when you need to do them, and the day will come
when you will be able to do the things you want to do
when you want to do them!

1

Ambition

What you get by reaching your destination is
not nearly as important as what you will become
by reaching your destination.

Motivation gets you going and habit gets you there.
Make motivation a habit and you will get there
more quickly and have more fun on the trip.

The basic goal-reaching principle is to understand
that you go as far as you can see, and when you
get there you will always be able to see farther.

You are the only one who can use your ability.
It is an awesome responsibility.

Ambition, fueled by compassion, wisdom and integrity,
is a powerful force for good that will turn the wheels
of industry and open the doors of opportunity
for you and countless others.

If we don't start, it's certain we can't arrive.

Obviously, there is little you can learn from doing nothing.

Attitude

Attitude

Positive thinking will let you use the abilities,
training and experience you have.

Positive thinking won't let you do anything but it will
let you do everything better than negative thinking will.

We all need a daily check up from the neck up
to avoid stinkin' thinkin' which ultimately leads
to hardening of the attitudes.

It's not what happens to you that determines how far you
will go in life; it is how you handle what happens to you.

You cannot tailor make the situations in life,
but you can tailor make the attitudes to
fit those situations before they arise.

Attitude

Of all the "attitudes" we can acquire,
surely the attitude of gratitude is the most important
and by far the most life changing.

When you choose to be pleasant and positive in the
way you treat others, you have also chosen,
in most cases, how you are going to be treated by others.

You can disagree without being disagreeable.

I've got to say no to the good so I can say yes to the best.

To respond is positive, to react is negative.

Encouragement

Encouragement

Start your child's day with love and encouragement
and end the day the same way.

You already have every characteristic necessary for success
if you recognize, claim, develop and use them.

You cannot make it as a wandering generality.
You must become a meaningful specific.

The best way to raise positive children in a negative world
is to have positive parents who love them unconditionally
and serve as excellent role models.

You will make a lousy anybody else,
but you will be the best "you" in existence.

You must manage yourself before you can
lead someone else.

Encouragement

When someone we love is having difficulty and is
giving us a bad time, it's better to explore the cause
than to criticize the action.

Take time to be quiet.

Obstacles are the things we see when we
take our eyes off our goals.

The best thing a parent can do for a child
is to love his or her spouse.

Your mate doesn't live by bread alone; he or she
needs to be "buttered up" from time to time.

Other people and things can stop you temporarily.
You're the only one who can do it permanently.

Guidance

Guidance

If you're sincere, praise is effective.
If you're insincere, it's manipulative.

Everybody says they want to be free. Take the
train off the tracks and it's free–but it can't go anywhere.

Many marriages would be better if the husband and wife
clearly understood that they're on the same side.

The more you express gratitude for what you have
the more you will have to express gratitude for.

Kids go where there is excitement.
They stay where there is love.

Duty makes us do things well,
but love makes us do them beautifully.

Guidance

It's not the situation, but whether we react (negative)
or respond (positive) to the situation that's important.

There's not a lot you can do about the national economy
but there is a lot you can do about your personal economy.

Lack of direction, not lack of time, is the problem.
We all have twenty-four hour days.

You can finish school, and even make it easy –
but you never finish your education, and it is seldom easy.

The best way to make your spouse and children
feel secure is not with big deposits in bank accounts,
but with little deposits of thoughtfulness
and affection in the "love account."

You've got to be before you can do,
and do before you can have.

All of us perform better and more willingly
when we know why we're doing what we have
been told or asked to do.

Money will buy you a bed, but not a good night's sleep,
a house but not a home, a companion but not a friend.

Most x-rated films are advertised as "adult entertainment,"
for "mature adults," when in reality they are juvenile
entertainment for immature and insecure people.

You don't drown by falling in water;
you only drown if you stay there.

When you give a man a dole you deny him his dignity, and
when you deny him his dignity you rob him of his destiny.

Remember, you can earn more money,
but when time is spent it is gone forever.

Happiness

I'm so optimistic I'd go after Moby Dick in a row boat
and take the tartar sauce with me.

Most of us would be upset if we were accused of being "silly."
But the word "silly" comes from the old English word
"selig," and its literal definition is "to be
blessed, happy, healthy and prosperous."

The chief cause of failure and unhappiness is trading
what you want most for what you want now.

Be helpful. When you see a person without a smile,
give him yours.

Hope

Hope

Our children are our only hope for the future,
but we are their only hope for their present and their future.

When you put faith, hope and love together
you can raise positive kids in a negative world.

Failure is an event, not a person.
Yesterday ended last night.

There are seldom, if ever, any hopeless situations,
but there are many people who lose hope
in the face of some situations.

You cannot solve a problem until you acknowledge
that you have one and accept responsibility for solving it.

Character gets you out of bed; commitment moves you
to action. Faith, hope, and discipline enable you
to follow through to completion.

The door to a balanced success opens widest
on the hinges of hope and encouragement.

16

Integrity

Character

Integrity / Character

If standard of living is your major objective,
quality of life almost never improves, but if quality of life
is your number one objective, your standard of living
almost always improves.

If people like you they'll listen to you,
but if they trust you they'll do business with you.

Ability can take you to the top,
but it takes character to keep you there.

The quality of a person's life is in direct proportion
to his or her commitment to excellence,
regardless of his or her chosen field of endeavor.

Keep your thinking right and your business will be right.

When a company or an individual compromises one time,
whether it's on price or principle,
the next compromise is right around the corner.

Integrity / Character

What you do off the job is the determining factor
in how far you will go on the job.

You build a successful career, regardless of your
field of endeavor, by the dozens of little things
you do on and off the job.

When you exercise your freedom to express yourself
at the lowest level, you ultimately condemn
yourself to live at that level.

With integrity you have nothing to fear,
since you have nothing to hide. With integrity
you will do the right thing, so you will have no guilt.
With fear and guilt removed you are
free to be and do your best.

When I discipline myself to eat properly, live morally,
exercise regularly, grow mentally and spiritually, and not put
any drugs or alcohol in my body, I have given myself the
freedom to be at my best, perform at my best,
and reap all the rewards that go along with it.

When we do more than we are paid to do,
eventually we will be paid more for what we do.

What comes out of your mouth
is determined by what goes into your mind.

You can get everything money will buy
without a lick of character, but you can't get
any of the things money won't buy—happiness,
joy, peace of mind, winning relationships, etc.,
without character.

Self-Image

If you don't like who you are and where you are,
don't worry about it because you're not stuck either
with who you are or where you are. You can grow.
You can change. You can be more than you are.

Some people find fault like there is a reward for it.

Far too many people have no idea of what they can do
because all they have been told is what they can't do.
They don't know what they want because
they don't know what's available for them.

Man was designed for accomplishment,
engineered for success, and endowed
with the seeds of greatness.

You were born to win, but to be the winner you were
born to be you must plan to win and prepare to win.
Then and only then can you legitimately expect to win.

When your image improves, your performance improves.

Self-Image

The greatest single cause of a poor self-image
is the absence of unconditional love.

It's not what you know, it's what you use
that makes a difference.

Success is not measured by what you do
compared to what others do, it is measured
by what you do with the ability God gave you.

Before you change your thinking,
you have to change what goes into your mind.

You are what you are and where you are because of what has
gone into your mind. You can change what you are and
where you are by changing what goes into your mind.

Don't be distracted by criticism. Remember –
the only taste of success some people have
is when they take a bite out of you.

Success

Success

Too many people spend more time planning how
to get the job than on how to become
productive and successful in that job.

You enhance your chances for success
when you understand that your yearning power
is more important than your earning power.

The price of success is much lower than the price of failure.

When management and labor (employer and employee)
both understand they are all on the same side,
then each will prosper more.

When we clearly understand that there is no superior sex
or superior race, we will have opened the door
of communication and laid the foundation
for building winning relationships with
all people in this global world of ours.

The only way to coast is down hill.

Remember there is plenty of room at the top –
but not enough to sit down.

Selling is essentially a transference of feeling.

If you will pump long enough, hard enough,
and enthusiastically enough, sooner or later
the effort will bring forth the reward.

You don't "pay the price" for success –
you enjoy the benefits of success.

Success is one thing you can't pay for. You buy it on the
installment plan and make payments every day.

Ability is important in our quest for success,
but dependability is critical.

Zig Ziglar
Biography

For over three decades Zig Ziglar has been
recognized by his peers as America's most
consistent messenger of hope and optimism.

Having shared the stage with Presidents Ford,
Reagan and Bush, Generals Norman Schwarzkopf
and Colin Powell, Dr. Norman Vincent Peale,
Paul Harvey and Dr. Robert Schuller, he is one of
the most sought after personal development
trainers in the world.

The client list of Ziglar reads like a who's who in
American and global business. Nine of his twenty-
three books have been on the bestseller lists and his
titles have been translated into more than thirty-
eight languages and dialects.

Zig has inspired people from every walk of life to
achieve more than they ever thought possible.

Ziglar VIP was created to address multiple training challenges that revolve around the efficacy of any program designed to increase productivity and performance.

A simple but effective gap analysis allows our developers to analyze and rank the needs in the organization. Classroom training can then be tailored to each corporation's key concerns. It is at this point that the Difference Maker Modules are prepared and scheduled to begin arriving in each participant's e-mail at pre-determined intervals.

RETENTION
Employees receive these DMMs weekly to enable them to practice learned skills. Delivered electronically to employees for 10 to 16 weeks, this recurring learning principle creates lasting habits.

ACCOUNTABILITY
Ensuring employees retain as much as possible of their training is an arduous task for an organization's leaders. Ziglar VIP, which encourages proactive employee/supervisor interactions, gives supervisors at-a-glance monitoring reports that let them know when to check in with employees.

VALUE
Training is a costly expense that can pay incredible dividends if strategically implemented. Ziglar VIP allows companies to target increased performance through the use of a proprietary web-based program, proven accountability model, and performance reporting.

Ziglar is dedicated to teaching high-performing companies how to lead with performance. Ziglar VIP is a revolutionary training tool that can be used to support any and all company training programs, regardless of the original training source.

For more information about how to put Ziglar VIP to work for your organization, call 800-527-0306.

ZIGLAR SALES SYSTEM

Ziglar Sales System teaches sales performance through an easy to-apply basic sales formula that is built on TRUST.

This adaptable program is performance-driven and can b utilized in any industry, with any product or service. Whe followed and applied, sales professionals can yield tremendou results in a remarkably short period of time.

For more information about Ziglar Sales System please vis us at www.ziglar.com/zss.

ESSENTIAL PRESENTATION SKILLS

Did you know that more people fear public speaking than fea death?

Ziglar's Essential Presentation Skills makes taking the leap easie and gives you trade secrets gleaned from one of America most beloved motivational presenters – Zig Ziglar. Essentia Presentation Skills improves sales performance, helps you thin "on your feet" in meetings and in front of a crowd, adds skills tha will enhance your career, improves closing ratios, and will mak all of your presentations more powerful.

For more information please visit us at www.ziglar.com/eps